THE INVISIBLE MAN

Kenny Abdo

Bolt!
An Imprint of Abdo Zoom
abdopublishing.com

abdopublishing.com

Published by Abdo Zoom, a division of ABDO, P.O. Box 398166, Minneapolis, Minnesota 55439. Copyright © 2019 by Abdo Consulting Group, Inc. International copyrights reserved in all countries. No part of this book may be reproduced in any form without written permission from the publisher. Bolt!™ is a trademark and logo of Abdo Zoom.

Printed in the United States of America, North Mankato, Minnesota.
052018
092018

THIS BOOK CONTAINS
RECYCLED MATERIALS

Photo Credits: Alamy, Everette Collection, iStock
Production Contributors: Kenny Abdo, Jennie Forsberg, Grace Hansen
Design Contributors: Dorothy Toth, Neil Klinepier

Library of Congress Control Number: 2017960603

Publisher's Cataloging-in-Publication Data

Names: Abdo, Kenny, author.
Title: The invisible man / by Kenny Abdo.
Description: Minneapolis, Minnesota : Abdo Zoom, 2019. | Series: Hollywood monsters | Includes online resources and index.
Identifiers: ISBN 9781532123191 (lib.bdg.) | ISBN 9781532124174 (ebook) | ISBN 9781532124662 (Read-to-me ebook)
Subjects: LCSH: Monsters & myths--Juvenile literature. | Monsters in literature-Juvenile literature. | Monsters in mass media--Juvenile literature.
Classification: DDC 398.2454--dc23

TABLE OF CONTENTS

THE INVISIBLE MAN

The Invisible Man is about a scientist named Dr. Jack Griffin. He makes a **formula** that turns his body completely invisible. When it cannot be reversed, he terrorizes a town with violence and mayhem.

The Invisible Man has become an **iconic** symbol in the horror **genre**.

ORIGIN

H.G. Wells was an English author famous for many popular novels. He wrote *The Time Machine*, *The Island of Doctor Moreau*, and *The Invisible Man* back-to-back.

THE INVISIBLE MAN

H.G. WELLS

He first wrote *The Invisible Man* in parts for Pearson's Weekly in 1897. It was published as a novel that same year.

Wells called his method of writing a "new system of ideas." He wanted the science in his books to be true. His stories would be scarier, because they were possible.

HOLLYWOOD

In 1933, the story revealed itself on the big screen. Claude Rains starred as the title character. It was his very first Hollywood **role**.

Even though he bombed the **audition**, Rains was hired. The director said, "I don't care what he looks like; that's the voice I want."

The Invisible Man is known for its inventive **visual effects**. Rains wore a full-body, black velvet suit when filming. Being **claustrophobic** made work difficult for him.

As the main character, Rains cannot be seen until the very last moment in the film.

The movie was a huge box office win! It was Universal Studios' most successful horror film since *Frankenstein*.

In 1940, *The Invisible Man Returns* was released. Because of the critical success, even more **sequels** were made after.

The Invisible Man has scared audiences in many other films, TV shows, and stage productions ever since.

21

GLOSSARY

audition – an interview for a job as an actor.

claustrophobia – extreme fear of small spaces.

formula – a mixture of liquids.

genre – a type of art, music, or literature.

icon – a person or thing regarded as a representative of something.

role – a part an actor plays.

sequel – a movie or other work that continues the story begun in a preceding one.

visual effect – an illusion created on-screen for a movie.

ONLINE RESOURCES

Booklinks
NONFICTION NETWORK
FREE! ONLINE NONFICTION RESOURCES

To learn more about The Invisible Man, please visit **abdobooklinks.com**. These links are routinely monitored and updated to provide the most current information available.

INDEX